When Love Begins

E.G.

BookLocker

Contents:

For Everyone Who Stayed.

Black = Lost

Welcome To Black:
Hello
This is Black
This is the furthest I have wandered from Hope
This is truth from a Depressed teen's perspective.

Wander with me.

An Introduction:
I am
A cracked mirror
Ink smudged fingerprints on clean cloth
Red blood on fresh snow
Shattered trust
I am
Back burner dreams
Burnt flowers disintegrating to ash
I am everything ruined
Stained
And abashed
Do not call me broken
Do not call me beautiful.

(I Am Not.)

E.G.

Outnumbered:
Who will help me?
I am falling
There are too many talking between my ears to hear
There are too many left in my heart to Love.

Steal Me Away:
Where did light go?
Don't they see my fright?
When it's here it's too bright
Alone again
Tired of knowing I'm myself
Take my sight
Stakes in the center of my irises would bleed less than I am
now
They would keep me from seeing this Night's mess
Tired of hearing obsessions with selfishness
Don't forgive me
I've given away whatever emotional muscle I may have gained
My workouts consist of curling empty cups
I'm working out how to bend my knees enough to crouch
below
Lonely's line of fire.

E.G.

Help:
She's hurting
Scraped open by memories
B l e e d i n g
I am not firmly enough in my body to be here
(Even for her)
I am not a big enough band aid
(Even covered in them)
To stick.

Naming Fears:
I am afraid of never being good enough
Or of always being too much
Or of falling in the permanently mundane in between
Lately, it's hard to find something that doesn't chill me
Cars
Lakes
Distance
Snakes
Empty mornings
Absent nights
Lonely afternoons
Secluded evenings
Heights
That's a new one
One I was never fearful of
Until I realized
I was terrified of myself
Falling still doesn't petrify me
The chance to jump does.

E.G.

Send Some Wind, I Don't Have The Lungs To Extinguish My
Life:
What is Suicide?
It is watching People around you hold candles
While blowing your own flame out.

Hiding (Hoping To Be Found):
It's my fault if I fall
For help too afraid to call
Worthless
Cover it
No one wants to see this
It's my fault when I fall.

E.G.

Stay Alive:
I hide in the shadows of false smiles
Barricading myself behind walls stitched together by the
thread of long sleeves
This is another ode to
Young lies
Growing up
Growing old
I haven't lived long enough to die
I've lived long enough to want to die
Let me stay happy
Please let me stay alive, alive.

I Won't Know Until I'm Shown:
Darkness inside and out
A lost soul ambushed by doubt
Sharp blades weren't around
I found a shard of dirty glass
(I threw that jagged blunder into the puddle we call a pond so
you wouldn't find my secrets leaked on it)
(Sorry)
Hands grasping weakly at frail hair
Being told
Life isn't fair
Doesn't prepare you
For a life that's unfair.

Try Again:
In the mirror
I lied and tried to reach perfect
In horror
I watched myself wave goodbye
To happiness
Reflection
Deceit
Inspection
Last night's scratches aren't up to scratch
This morning's weigh in doesn't measure up
Tomorrow demands
Try Again.

Too Late:
Too late
Too late
Too late
I'm sorry I'm impatient
But I can't shake the terror that time is running out
I don't want to learn to wait
There's another load of Self-Hate
Building up in my chest
Please, please
Don't lie to me
I'm a waste of space
Yes, even at my best
The rest is simply stupid
What else is new?
Should I have hidden?
Put my fragments in a box
Seal the lid
You'd all be better without me around
Don't deny it
I've seen the judgmental frowns.

Tortured Artist:
Empty skin for a canvas
Empty promises for paint
Empty blades for brushes
Empty soul full of hate.

Break, Breaking, Broken:
Not until I'd crashed into a smattering of shadow particles
On the triangle rocks that live at the foot
Of the cliff that is Depression
Did I realize how far I'd fallen.

Flounder In Sand, Step On Water:
Drowning in the shallows of the world
The deep end
Isn't as fun as it looks
From shore
The shore
Isn't as solid as it looks
From the deep end.

Remote Control, Remotely Removed:
I only say wrong things
What's the point?
Mostly cram my head
Chalk full of
Sad songs
Grey and blue
Charcoal drawings
I've never liked grey
Now it's all I see
Turn irrational without cause
Wishing that life would pause until I'm ready for it
I need a remote to Love
Rewind you saying
I Love you
Until I believe it
You're so far
I'm so stuck here
Remove me from this waste bin
Steal my pen when you steal my joy
Take everything if you're going to take anything
I'd rather plummet
Than stand on the edge
Of another Goodbye
Losing control of my lung's intake when I cry
Would you rather hyperventilate or suffocate?
Would you rather live feeling like a cadaver
Or die?

He Was A Blizzard:
Promises
Dropping into my hair
Sticking like snowflakes
Clinging to my eyelashes like tears
I can imagine the sour taste of deceit from here
Cloud particles have never hit my soul this heavily before
You keep saying it
But you didn't Love me.

You Should Have Believed Me When I Told You I Was A
Paradox Girl, I Meant It:
Quit calling yourself stupid
I know I do the same
But I can't watch while someone else
Treats them self
The way I treat myself
That's the hypocritical paradox of the Depressed
You don't have to be alone
(I am alone)
You don't have to be Sad
(I am nothing but)
It's okay.
(It is not okay.)

Purple And Blue Babies:
Bruised kids
Cannot count
The number of times
They've fallen asleep
Accompanied by the jarring rhythm
Of hideous words
And the discordance
Of shouting voices
Eventually
That much noise
Causes a ringing in their ears
They hear it long after the noise has faded
Cocking heads
At each raise of tone
Resounding echoes of their younger years
An interference with here and now
Deafening verbal violence
Beats the tempo on influenced eardrums
Drowning out softer sounds
It's Hard To Grow Up When All You Hear Is Your Childhood.

Tragedy Taking Care Of Tragedies:
She swept herself away with other People's Sadness
Until she couldn't find her own
When she finally remembered
She was a tragedy too
Is there one main character to be found here
Or two?

Circles:
Lie
Smile
Scratch
Cut
Anxiety takes the form of a stone in your gut
Cry
Scream
Sleep
Bleed
Who said I'd never be good enough?
Shut up!

Every Word Is A Stone, Every Stone Leaves A Mark:
Insides crumbling
Every time a rock is thrown
I collapse
Lately
Everything is a rock
I spend every day
Walking to and from interior repairs
Trying to prop myself up from the inside
I can't fill myself
These hollow spaces
Are caving in.

E.G.

Girl:
Past of broken promises.
See?
Telltale tracks of red ink on her paper white skin.
See?
Glass box is clear, but keeps you from getting close.
See?
You're blocked out.
See?
She's locked in.
See?

Stronger:
Who has not Loved at least once?
Who has not had their heart fractured at least once?
If you exist
Show me how to be
As invincible as you are.
(I cannot find a trustworthy way to protect this soft organ.)

Unrelated Randomness:

Words
dancing through my head
A song.

You
resonating in my ears
A gong.

Scars
Climbing across my skin
Too long.

Me
Incessantly wishing
To be gone.

Frost Is Pulverized Glass From Heaven:
Pale girls draped in long sleeves and forced laughs
Are not
What hidden knives
Stale words
And Regret
Look like
Smothering, choking
Smoke is too heavy
To settle on already shaking shoulders
He can't carry you
Is it too much?
Snowflakes of glass
Cutting as they slide past
A stinging in the eyes
Opaque and foreign gaze
From secrets too long kept
Imagine angels with hammers
Smashing up the window panes
We look through
Too afraid to remove.

E.G.

We Are Poorly Packaged Heirlooms:
Porcelain children
Scarlet cracks tracing every curve and smile
Shaken on the way to being an adult
We're already trembling too violently
To arrive at our destination unhurt
Handle Us With Care
Fragile
Keep Face Up
The workers must have been blind
They must have stumbled
When they delivered us.

Bleeding Through Midnight, Bleeding Through Noon:
I don't see the magic tonight
Perhaps I only ever imagined I could
I can't find myself in this light
Why don't you all stop saying I should ?
I am bleeding through midnight
A frightening place to be
It reminds me of a phantom
I happened once to see
It was a phantom
That looked like me
Sometimes I wish I could leave
Find someplace to be free
But what's the use in freedom if memories never flee ?
Darkness only gets thicker
The voices attack
Biting, quicker
Dad, won't you ever stop
Fighting, working, hurting
To realize you have daughters and sons ?
Is it too late to Love me ?

E.G.

Who Is To Say What Matters And What Doesn't:

They're just scratches. They don't mean anything.

Liar. They mean everything.

Say You Love Me, Cut Me Again (Before I Cut Myself Again):
Words are knives
They can be used to fight for others
Or to hurt them
But don't underestimate their ability to cut
They stab deeper than can be seen
I've never met someone
Who's held me more firmly spellbound
Maybe it's because
No one is you
Maybe it's because
I'm still new to looking for Love
I don't know about you
But I'm satisfied to end looking
Right here
If you want to
If you want me to
I'll be true.

Why Does So Much Sadness Occur In Bathrooms Pt. I:
That girl
Is another Sad story
Heart breaks at the lines of crimson on her thigh
The bathroom sink is ruined and bloody
Desperation to escape
I am begging you
Don't go yet
Don't say goodbye.

My Body Is Depression's Favorite Costume:
There are ghosts who slumber at the foot of my bed
Who wander noisily on the interior of my head
Killing from the inside out
Forcing tears unshed
Unzipping the back of my skull
To climb inside
(They've left a rip in the grey matter)
(It's dripping into my vision. Everything is covered in film)
(Hurry)
(If you hurry you can stop my runny mess before I've leaked
out)
(If you hurry you can rescue me)
Spending every day and night
Laughing at my marionette strings
Tied to their phantom fingers
Stealing control
Gamboling, they think it's funny how weak they've starved me
into being
(This girl is no longer a being)
(She is an abandoned house)
(Her eyelashes are fences of caution tape)
(Her eyes are an overgrown lawn full choked daisies)
(This possessed property hasn't seen spring since it started
pouring pain)
I watch, cowed and cowering, as they gamble my last play at
life
For a few more cigarette shaped slices up my forearm
This is a jungle gym they invite their Demon friends to swing
from
It opened for the publicity of friends' caring camera recorded
newspaper reels last year

E.G.

I am reduced to a peeling flower in the patterned wallpaper
Pasted to the inside of my decaying cranium
Glued, stuck, wasted.
Get out.
Let me go.

God, Please, Not One More:
One more lie
Another care thrown out
Apathy is a state of existence
It began with fear
One more scratch
It's just another cut
They know you're hurt
But
One more day of deceit
Mother, cousins, friends
Not as good a liar as you think you are
Stop letting them see through
One more secret
Can you keep it?
Let's test
How many Steine *a girl can carry*
Before she throws them down
Or sinks.

E.G.

You Don't Belong And You Know It:
Dead soul of a living girl
This house is for the living and newly born
What is it doing here?
What are you doing here?

I Haven't Won A Fight I Can Remember:
Mouth open in silent scream
Head stuck inside a dream
Hands clenched tight
Losing another fight
Eyes blurred
Absurd
Stomach starving
Body dying
Mind gave up on trying
Destruction is a hurried process
(There are more People than you waiting to want to die.)

E.G.

Razor Blades Are Nothing Compared To Lies:
Skin
Shredding like paper
Beneath words.
(It's not your fault I'm not trying.)

I'm No Carpenter
But I'll Saw A Trap Door In Your Poisoned Soul
And Build A Ladder To The Ground
If It Will Help You Escape Yourself:

His mind is the prison where he hides
Mistakenly thinking it an escape.

Boy,
Almost Man.

I Know
I Understand
I don't have to be in your head
To know what you're feeling.

Falling is Falling,
No matter what or who pushed you over the edge
Lies are Lies,
No matter who told them
Sinking is Sinking,
No matter what is dragging you down.

I have been there too.

E.G.

Completed Project Of Ruination:
Blood rolls down wrist
Hand hardens into fist
Eyes fogged with mist
Heart adrift
Structure shaking
So is mine
Can't you hear the rumbling?
Gears of insanity grumbling
The voices are nearly done
This was a solo task
I mastered it.
(I learned over dramatization too.)

Another Metaphor Involving Glass:
People
Are glass
Hitting each other the wrong way
Everything shatters
I'm still stepping on shards
I keep finding glimmers of him
Embedded in my heels and palms
Why couldn't I feel the splinters digging in when he held my
hand ?
I'm stepping on sore soles
Bleeding through my socks
Trying to walk away
Every movement hurts
When will I be able to leave
Without ripping my skin to bits ?

Understand:
I only choose to hurt
When I can choose to.

E.G.

A Fatal Flaw:
To give them everything or nothing at all.

There's No Difference Between His Smiles And Frowns (He's
Always Sad):
His smiles are stillborn
Dead before they reach frigid air
He's living upside down
Grim lips
He won't allow himself to feel
Because he grew up
Hearing that he felt too much.

E.G.

Untitled (I Can't Name What Never Was):
My Love is lost in tears and blood
There are now only scars
To show what could have been.

Walls Are Built To Keep Things Out:
These children don't know the swallowing darkness
On the other side of the door
I beg them
Stop peering through the lock
They will find you soon enough
Run while you're innocent and young
The mire will age you
It leaves lines in your face and arms
You can't erase the marks.

From: Me
To: Myself
Subject: Warning

Dear Heart,

Stop thinking of yourself in poetry.

You are nothing that beautiful.

      Sincerely,
            A Concerned Friend

Sad, Pitiful, Kid:
I want to give up
Without the guilt that always follows
There are more nights than not
When I'd rather run in front of a car
Than live long enough to learn to drive one.

E.G.

Sheets & Sickness:
I am sick & disgusted
With myself
For not being skinny & pretty enough
Then I am shallow & despicable for letting that be important
It's not supposed to be this hard to swallow
But it is.
I'm so tired of this.

Drip, Drop, Drip (Drop):
I shouldn't miss you
I know what you think of me
I know you think I can't keep my mouth shut
I hope you can hear me say
I wouldn't have told them
What you said
That was for you & me
I am sorry
I couldn't halt the puddles and pools of
Hopeless
Infringing on my mind
I am sorry
I got your carpet damp
With my stormy aversion to promises & trust
I have clouds tied on strings & attached to my wrists
They've asked me to join them in the sky again & again
For you
Again & again
I told them
No
But now they're crying in the kitchen & den
Our books are getting wet
Our pots and pans are hiding in their cupboards to stifle the
din
They don't have hands to mop up their natural disasters
I am tired of being on my hands & knees
& you are gone
So
Next time they beg me to float on air currents with them
I think
I'll grab on

E.G.

Say
Yes
& lift off.

We're Looking At Me Through Opposite Ends Of A Tunnel,
We're Blocking The Exits:
What can you see here that's worth those tears?
A paper towel roll is a telescope to a round trip view of
imagination
My tunnel vision blocks everything but the circle I see of you
You're a bright spot
You're hiding everything behind you
You're you and couldn't be more unhappy you are
You're you and I couldn't be happier you are.

A Night In The Forest Of My Heart:
Gaps on my arm are filled
I don't have a map to navigate the night
I've mistaken my Swiss army knife of Depressed tactics
For a tool to mark my journey here
Scraped off scabs like bark
Counted scars like constellations
Carved the Polaris Bear into my left arm
The Great Square of Pegasus into my right
My hips are Castor and Pollux
Matching twin disasters
My tongue is broken twig, cricket leg
It only knows how to snap
It only knows how to ask for company once it's dark
I pulled on and laced up trek boots
Will firm tread help me combat these Demonic dryads?
Woodland spirits sneak under underbrush
Surprise ambush from behind burning bushes
Poison ivy, poison oak
Some People perpetuate the idea that Virginia Creeper is a
figment of the imagination
The existence of Mental Illness is a perpetual presence
It's here
I whisper
It's growing in your backyard, in the garden of your mind
Pull it out
Kill it before it overtakes your lawn, your life.

I Am Not Listened To Nor Am I Unheard:
Why am I destroying myself
For rules I don't have to abide by?
There's no need to lie
Crying for help that won't come
When the deed is done
I'm not better
I'm just numb.

Stop It, Stop It, Stop It:

I am not beautiful.

Stop.

Black (Continued)

Sorry:
We have to fall into another valley
Before we are strong enough to climb up the next cliff.

(Don't) Fall with me.

Juvenile Psych Ward Pt. I:
Blue pajamas
Cold floor
Too many pills equal locked doors
Questions asked
I kept up my mask
A roommate who was diving and ducking past the young girl
she was
Curly headed boy who I could have Loved anywhere but in
that hospital
Short haired, Sad, Sad, Sad, girl who is Sad still
1, 2, 3, 4th floor
Distant from everything familiar, but you can't get away from
yourself
Certain place for uncertain adolescents
A Home unto itself
I didn't want to say goodbye
Ready to leave until I left
A farewell to more than fellow patients
We needed each other
Though we only had one another for a week and a half
At most
Indescribable atmosphere
A dimension where it's assumed you want to die
Most have tried to
A crowd of miserable
Immaturely aged
We Loved with a hopeless Love
That knows affection is unbelievable
But can't help itself from natural human instinct
Tearing open our wrists under tables
Stealing paper clips so your new friend won't do the same

E.G.

Hypocritical, incapable, and marrow deep Sad
I won't forget the place where pencils aren't allowed without
supervision
And ways to end your life
Are discussed without tension and as openly as this season's
hairstyles
Nonchalant death wishes have been with us too long
Suicide pacts
Were how we got along
(Shh, we weren't supposed to)
Throwing up, I couldn't stop her
It tore me apart
'til I learned to do the same
Strangle yourself in the shower
I know this is sickening
I'm sorry
This is what it is
I will not beautify an ugly thing.
Crushed:
Do you understand yet?
It's difficult to breathe
Under the weight of myself.

Learning The Hard, Hard, Hard Way:
If you don't listen you'll have to learn the hard way
I thought I was trying to listen
I didn't realize my ears were bleeding next to deaf and dumb
rocks on the ground
Van Gogh doppelgänger
Diagnosing myself with Mental Illness is my newest Love
Here's another body part for your experiment
Here's my handicapped heart
Wait, Hold On
How many calories are in a tablespoon of yellow paint?
If it's more than what's in one of peanut butter I can't swallow
it
Does acrylic sunshine have to stay down to work?
Fingers scratch if they can't find my throat after a bite has
slipped past
(Not many bites have slipped past since It began)
When you've sliced up your reality processing canal
Bashed the drum Honesty beats it's tune on
Online quizzes sound the same as a shrink's questions
I already knew what he was analyzing me to find
Clinical Depression
Ugh, please
It's supposed to be
Severe Clinical Depression
He said
You're showing signs of a developing Eating Disorder
Dude, I already labeled myself Anorexic
(I'm well aware I don't look like one yet. Wait for it. I'm
getting there)
Depression pulled my skin taut
Anxiety held a scimitar

E.G.

We are the only ones who can hear you now
We are the only ones you can hear.

Absence Of Substance = Presence Of Death:
The world is tipping
I can't find a place to stand without slipping
Everything black
Caused by the meals I've skipped
I lost control
Trying to take control
Deprived myself of salvation
By restricting food
This is bigger than my shaking hands
This is called starvation.

E.G.

I Don't Remember The Label On The Bottle, I Remember The
Results Of The Google Search:
Tattooed with a history of Self-Hate
It's a mystery I'm still alive
I knew what was in that bottle
Too Sad to wait
Scared
I fabricated more problems
When I ran from the plate.

What A Shame, She Was So Young:
Will I ever be good enough?
Never.
NEVER
never
Never!
Never
But raise your head, Honey
Force a smile, pretend to be tough
Look up at your stars for the last time
They've never Loved you back
Welcome an untimely death.

E.G.

(Suicide By Starvation):
The only thing passing these chapped lips
      (Chapped because water weighs too much to drink)
Is gift wrapped lies
Ana (orexia)
Maps out how many calories I'm allowed each day
Cheeks rarely dry
She shapes my thoughts like they've always been hers
      (If there was a space they weren't, remind me of it)
You'll never be skinny if you eat that way
Please, don't ask why
I don't know how to fight
A body fighting itself to say goodbye.

Juvenile Psych Ward Pt. II:
Plastic bed frame
No hangers in the closet
Nothing sharp on your person
Long sleeves, Please
You are a trigger warning
From the window in my shared room
I could see a building across the street
I counted the windows up and down
It would have been high enough
(*For what?*)
(Jumping, Stupid)
Search engines told me that weeks before
I was a Suicidal girl
Staring at what could have ended me
Through two inch thick glass
Across an oblivious road
Because what was meant to finish me hadn't done its job
Imagining the way down
(Thanks for trying, Nurses, but America's Funniest Videos
weren't so funny there)
My roommate and I talked about ghosts and why we were
there the first night
Dutch blitz, drama, and swear words almost every curfew
after
I hope residential treated her well
I don't expect to see her again
I don't need to
She belonged to that phase of life
We are living in different times.

A Brief Rundown Of The Kids I Met In The Inpatient Living Room:
She was the fifth 14 year old to arrive that week
He, on purpose, crashed his car
She had been there twice before
He was a high school athletic star
(I saw your arm, Jock. That will leave a scar)
She had an amazing laugh
He, brown eyes, a singer's name, guitar player
She was a passed around foster kid
He flashed good nature under glasses and a mop of curly hair
She was a teenage tattoo artist
(Sharpie puzzle pieces on your arm will scrub off, Girl. What's underneath won't. It won't piece you back together)
The only thing lumping every kid on that floor together
Were the feelings that got us there
Was waiting to get out.

Folded Squares Of Paper And Filthy Sinks Are Where I Spit
My Secrets:
Napkins wadded up with secrets
Freezing, freezing hands
Buzzing ears, darkness whenever you stand
Counting, Counting, Counting
Always counting to quell your fears
Except
It spurs an Anorexic's fears
Don't you dare swallow that!
Spit it out!
Purge until you see blood.

EDs Should Be Considered Self-Mutilation:
I hate my stomach and my thighs
Crooked teeth, exhausted lies
I'm not losing weight quickly enough to satiate Ana
To keep going
Throwing up everything I eat
It's okay, right?
I still have a Self-Harm clean streak.

The Truth Terrifies:
They're saying I'm worth it
They're saying they Love me and care
Do you think telling them I haven't eaten in three days
Would scare them away?

Sorry, Mom:
I didn't participate in dinner again tonight
I know I'm a sinner
That I'm letting Them beat me
But in the heat of a moment
All I can think is
Knife, knife, knife
I need a knife
In the middle of strife all I hear is
Don't ever eat
They're yelling at me
You don't deserve anything but pain
You'll always feel the same.

Wish I Could Wish To Be Here:
I'm going to shrink in front of you
The only thing I'll fight is the People who say they Love me
Don't drink your calories!
Is only one of my million rules
I don't have an ounce of control
(Or water)
Don't follow my role
Dinner rolls are forbidden
This is how an ED rolls
Clothes aren't falling off
That means I haven't suffocated enough fat
To make them loose
So much more weight to lose
Tape measure noose
I wish it were a noose instead of a tape measure
I wish numbers weren't chasing my Self-Control
I wish my body were anything but what it is
I wish wishes meant something
I wish I believed living is worth this.

E.G.

Quiet:
I get it
I'm a freak
No, please, don't ask
I haven't eaten this week
I know they'll see this
As attention seeking
Don't ever let your secrets leak
Ana says to keep starving until I'm skinny or dead
You can't save me from myself
I'll put my feelings on my mental shelf
He said
Tie a noose out of thread and bleed bright red.

Wavering Walls:
The bricks building the walls that keep me sane
Shake with every word she says
Screaming floods my thoughts in her wake.

Death Is A Game Master:
Beat me up
I'm in a mood to be reckless
Downing a bottle, unidentified contents
Jumping off a bridge
Don't check for rocks
I don't want to know it won't work
Sliding a knife across my skin several thousand times
Bruise me, Bruise me, Bruise me
I'm numb
Give me anything
As long as it's real
Make me be Here
Highway spirits
Windows and guard rolled down
Fold up your sleeves and kiss me
Pull over
Screech, Scream, Teach me something new
Why am I responsible for our pace?
We are a cliff face
Let me Leap
Let me play games with Death until he wins.

You Should See Me The Way I See Myself:
Body Dysmorphia
Or Disgusting Truth ?
They run together across stones of failing survival tips
I can't tell water from poison
Both weigh too much in my stomach to stay there
I threw away my canteen and silverware miles ago
What is the point in carrying something I am unable to use ?
(What is the point in carrying on when I am unusable ?)
Just
Tell me
I am who I think I am
And I will permanently leave you alone
Just
Tell me
This is what matters
And I will be ten steps ahead of those words leaving your
mouth
Just
Tell me
It is time to go
And I am gone yesterday .

I Am Aware This Page Is Not Poetry (Forgive Me, I Am
Desperate For A Reply):
Were They Right To Leave ?
Were They Right To Leave ?
Were They Right To Leave ?
Were They Right To Leave ?
Were They Right To Leave ?
Were They Right To Leave ?
Were They Right To Leave ?
Were They Right To Leave ?
Were They Right To Leave ?
Were They Right To Leave ?
Were They Right To Leave ?
Were They Right To Leave ?
Were They Right To Leave ?
Were They Right To Leave ?
Were They Right To Leave ?
Were They Right To Leave ?
Were They Right To Leave ?
Were They Right To Leave ?
Were They Right To Leave ?
Were They Right To Leave ?
Were They Right To Leave ?
Were They Right To Leave ?
Were They Right To Leave ?
Were They Right To Leave ?
Were They Right To Leave ?
Were They Right To Leave ?
Were They Right To Leave ?
Were They Right To Leave ?
Were They Right To Leave ?
Were They Right To Leave ?

Were They Right To Leave ?
Were They Right To Leave ?
Were They Right To Leave ?
Were They Right To Leave ?
Were They Right To Leave ?
Were They Right To Leave ?
Were They Right To Leave ?
Were They Right To Leave ?
Were They Right To Leave ?
Were They Right To Leave ?
Were They Right To Leave ?
Were They Right To Leave ?

E.G.

Am I Here Or Am I In My Head:
I am not real
I am not alive tonight
I like it this way
But
I like it this way.

Why Does So Much Sadness Occur In Bathrooms Pt. II:
She spits into the bathroom sink
Hands smell like despair
Brain dwelling on bad memories
On People who said they cared
Though it's too soon to tell
She doubts she will ever be well.

E.G.

Don't Write About Me, It Would Take Up More Space:
I want to be the type of girl
Poetry is written about
But I'm not
I'm not
I'm not.

(I Am Not.)

Friendship Pt. I:

I've lost my grip on it.

She's A Discouraged Disappointment (Careful, Your Teenager
Is Showing):
It's dangerous when I get like this
Consumed ironically by apathy
Forget to brush my hair
To eat
(That isn't forgetfulness)
This beat matches my still pounding heart
Disappointing
You ?
Or that you're still alive ?
Forget to sleep
Too tired to weep.

Iceberg Girl, Frozen Touch:
The scars on my arms are fading
I'm wading out to sea
Ha!
They can't check
Nobody knows when my hips bleed
Her lips are chapped and impossible to read
This game is
(Isn't)
Far from over
How many moves have I got left?
He calls my name
Glances past
Doesn't see the slit veins hiding under this mask
Last night was hard
The next will be worse
She fills up her liquor cup to try and quench the thirst
The first cut is the deepest
That is a lie
Do they know how fast the knife can fly?
I won't deny I'm a mess
Everyone can plainly see it
Though not everyone senses the depth.

E.G.

Unmarred Is A Foreigner, Unscarred Is A Stranger:
I don't remember
Who I was before the first intentional scrape happened
What did I look like before Sadness?
This madness is staining my perception red and black
Happiness scares me
So do You
Good things never last.

Who Does She Think She Is:
She hurt others by hurting herself
She doesn't understand how she could mean enough to be
able to hurt them
Caring has to be in place
For actions to cut.

Trust Me, You Don't Want Me:
I am not a nice Girl
My hands are cooler than ice
I clumsily misplace fragments of myself
Dropping on either side like grains of rice
A shake
A roll
The dice tells me how to be
I'm not trying to not listen
Toss over wads of salvation
Wrap me in gauze of honest truth
Cover my ears when my wrists are bound by my own
hindering stubbornness
If you're willing
(If you'd like to)
(If you wouldn't mind)
Love Me.
With your whole heart
Mine is already
(Has long been)
Yours.
(Who am I kidding? Read the title of this page. Don't be
dumb. Believe It.)

Scar Tissue Paper:
I'll follow the words
Until I'm hollow
Emptied onto a page
Covered in black lines
That match the red ones on my hips
Carved by rage.

E.G.

Build An Umbrella For Me, I Am Raining:
Don't help me
I'm not fighting
I'm not trying
Why am I not trying?
Crying only helps for intervals
Where, when did it all go wrong?

Almost Numb:
I'm not hungry
That's deceit
It's always asked
Why?
Because I'm sick in the head
(To what lengths would you go to die?)
My Mother yells like thunder
I'm told I should be fine
I want to be seven feet under with no sky
I am hideous
Red tracks running down my thighs
They'll be horrified when I step into the light
Voices handing me a gun and pills
Oh my, God
Ribbon tied like a noose
Perfect bundle to try
As a bird I could ride on the wind
I'd leave this place
Don't wait up for me tonight
(Or any other)
(Pretend I'm gone until I am)
The twitch of his mouth is slight
I cry too much
My chest is tight
When will I learn to shut up, sit down, and not defy?
There's a ringing in my ear
What's it like to get high?
Quit bringing me new mistakes
I'll have to be sly
I hide until I'm too ashamed to say goodbye.

A Week Of Empty Results In A Weak Mind:
Sometimes she goes for days without eating
She's fond of the saying
Cheaters never win
But longs to skip to the end of her life
She doesn't want to fight to find sleep
Another miserable night.

Exhausted Avalanche Of Emotions:
I am too tired to keep climbing
Ritualistic rites threaten to push me out of the passenger seat
I spiral past
Picking up speed
Tumbling over mountainsides
Have I gone write
Or have I fallen behind?
If you know where I've gone
Point me in the right direction
Push me after myself before I'm lost from sight.
(From life.)

Don't Ask If You Aren't Prepared For The Answer:
Counting crimson lines
Along with calories
What's the amount of strokes you've laid on yourself?
(I'm tempted to tell you)
You don't want to know
Why ask?
He won't look me in the eyes if I show him
Attention Slut
Sure
Stares paralyze me
I'm useless in public
(And everywhere else)
You're all I think I need
Leave me alone
Okay
I hear you
I'm gone.

Morning Reveals Night Madness:
Self-Destruction is on
Flip the switch before dawn comes
Save me from the mess before it happens
Keep the shades drawn
Don't let the sun shine on what I've done
I'm afraid of what I will say to me.

Emotionally Impaired:
She screams and roars I don't understand
Oblivious to the knife already in hand
Blind to sick scarlet shades tainting my mind
This isn't what I planned for tonight
Deaf to the pleas she sends through loud arguments and quiet
Love
Verbal friction rubs my wrists raw
By this time
The store of band aids under my bed is sizable
Indifferent to the fight I know is coming next
After three thousand cuts
Rolling drops of blood painted too many tracks on my arm to
still catch me off guard
The sting isn't surprising anymore.

Anticipation:
She's tip toeing to the dresser drawer before reaching the
stairs
She's climbing the stairs before she's awake
She's walking into that room
Locking the door
Holding the blade like it's air
They cry every time she leaves
They know without knowledge
The lies have ordered
That she bleed to breathe.

E.G.

Idle Hearts Fall Ill:
Late nights
Blurry words
Lights too bright
Swords too sharp
Red marks on blue wrists
Are those new or old?
Hurry
Find something for my cavernous heart to do
Dizzy
I must keep my hands busy and off that drawer knob
I am not alright.

What I Have Done:
I'm so sorry.
Are you apologizing to yourself or them?

Depression:
Bigger than routine Sadness
Numbness longing for pain
Melancholic madness
Transforming
I Love you
Into
I'm lying
All your useless head does is request to death
Crying on the bathroom floor at 2:00 p.m. and again at a.m.
Blood dripping down your wrist both times from the amount
of hate you're holding inside
At yourself
It's Not Right, You're Right
It has to bust out somehow
Loathing the pattern and person you're living in
Should I make a list of the things wrong with me?
Nah
It'd be way too long
Gripping your sides, pinching
All you see, think, and feel is
Fat
Do they know you threw up breakfast again this morning?
Shh, don't tell them that!
Fighting Demons constantly
Sometimes you win
Sometimes you lose
Forcing you to choose
Cut, purge, starve, or die?
There's no one to catch you when you take the leap
You have no wings
I've sliced them off

No means to fly
He asked
Is this every other day for you?
I lied and said yes
I'm too scared to tell him what it's really like with no end in
sight
Depression is a Monster with a capital D
Especially tonight.

E.G.

Still Leaking Stupid Hope:
I don't blame him for anything
Pulling sleeves down in shame
He never notices
Or if he does, he's never brave enough to say
It's the price I pay for romantic ignorance
I don't care
(You can grab me and wring how much I care out of my tear
soaked hair.)
(Please do.)
(Wring Me Dry Of Him.)

Clamber Clumsily:
I climb up
And slip down
Don't frown at me like that
I know
I deserve no crowns.

E.G.

Long Distance, Sinking Ship:
Overdose to see
The ones I miss most
Ironic consequences
Taking me farther
From the ones I miss most
I can't feel myself being held close anymore
Could I ever?
Distance is called a killer
I wish it were as lethal as every mile and moment feel
Far from him
For better or worse
We're over
It was a childish trip to him and back
I'm glad I am glad we're done.

A Fortnight Of Throwing Up Whole Meals Leaves A Hole In
Your Connection To Anything Holy:
I'm at the two week mark
But I'm one pound behind
I can't see this ending until I'm laid in the ground
As cold as always, and not only in my mind
What's the plan?
Don't Eat
I guess that's simple enough
My breathing gets rough now and then
Like there are holes being worn in my lungs
My heart doesn't like to beat firmly as it should
But hey, I'm finally beginning to be thin
My head spins, blackness consumes
As soon as it passes I resume spitting out food
Ringing ears
Bringing back when I did this before
When I said I never would again
The longer I last without eating
(It's longer each relapse)
The further I grow from remembering
Who I was
When I was more than this.

E.G.

Leave Me Alone:
Shaking
Tired of waking as myself
Others don't see what I do
They think they can make me eat
Why don't they understand
Healthy meat on my bones
Is the furthest from what I want to be?
A concave stomach is what Ana says I need to be happy
You haven't given me a better answer than that so
I'll keep trusting her instructions
Until you do.

I'm Lost If I'm Not Lost:
I have to cross the line that looks like danger
(Don't hold me back)
Ana's anger shows when the scale stays the same
I'll risk everything to be her number
Is everything a game?
I'm running out of moves to play.

She:
I can't help her or hold her when I'm here
She was shaking
Can you taste fear?
Tear bright eyes make me look twice
Waking us up to the fact
She's Not Alright
The plan slid awry tonight
Burning our plane wings
Plummet
You think she's fake?
If you'd seen the cuts
Or shivered in the dark and cold
You wouldn't be so bold.

We're Never Too Old To Cry:
Living presses heavily on young shoulders
Giving fills the cracks in my cement grey brain
Tumbling downhill faster than crumbling boulders
Somebody catch me
This is a trust fall
See, if you do it just to be watched
They'll only call your name out loud in whispers of mockery
You must find the footholds on your own
And if you manage to stick the landing
Don't you dare get cocky!
It's still your fault that you fell
Now there's a mountain standing in your shadow
Waiting to be climbed
Careful
It will laugh when you slip back
Into hating the color of her lips because
They remind you of the first sip of wine
Grading into
A first kiss
Look at yourself
(I hate looking at myself)
He'll never want to say
She's mine.

Drowned In Thirst:
Anorexia is in control
I crave the end more than I crave a guiltless bite
(I would give anything for a mouthful I didn't hate myself
during/after)
Is starvation at last taking its toll?
I'm not meant for this
I can't play this role any longer
What are my lines?
No, not the ones under my sleeves
Feed me a cue
(But nothing else)
Does anyone else think in rhymes?
Poetry clogs emotional arteries
Girl lost to
(Too)
Deep.

Strolling On A Sword Tip, Walking On Worry:
Dim light is bright here
I am busy existing on edges
A part of me wants to be fought for
The rest has been ready to pledge my short life to the grave
Testing severely Suicidal limits
Is the only time I near brave
You might mean it when you say you Love me
You can't save me from this.

Then vs. Now:
God
Another relapse
I wonder if he remembers lying on our backs in the grass
Before I wanted to kill myself
Before he ran away
To warning signs I was deaf
Is that why he left ?
My hands are shaking, empty
I'm not the same person I was yesterday
I pester and question
My thoughts are lumps of half formed, overused clay
Bumping into each other
If I were skinnier I wouldn't be in your way
Cutting Isn't The Answer
Neither Is Not Eating
Watch the lines and emptiness
They're feeding Demons
Oops, I'm bleeding
Last week he kept them at bay
But tonight, again, I'm lonely
There is no one but me to blame
Where did I go ?
Will I always be the same ?
Where will I be tomorrow ?
Sitting pitifully in Sad
Nothing is gone but one
(One was everything. Everything is gone with one)
It's my fault
I have nothing left to say.

Whirlpool:
Fighting, fighting, fighting
Words set my heart ablaze
Brazen voices shouting
Lighting up the wrong way
Can you see the stars?
Certain nights
They're all that's mine
Did you drink the whole bottle?
Did it work?
Send the formula to being numb
Feeling nothing hurts
Feeling this is worse
Would you rather that I burst
Or let the pain bleed out?
I rain with thunder
Or starve in a drought
Pumping arms to not be sucked under
Please
Not Again
I'm useless
Dreams full of him
I should have been someone different
I didn't know how to change colors then
Now I can't find the brake
Take me back to when we were friends.

Unsolicited Solitude:
You said you wanted to help
I wanted to believe it
If you did
Where are you now?
How do I trust when others have left, slamming the door?
My frames are still settling from the most recent exit
Wasting another night, pulled apart
This floor knows my shape better than I know it myself
Thanks, Body Dysmorphia
Your collapse of me is a job thoroughly done
I've never had a more consistent friend
Unless you count your cousin Depression
Anxiety and I are acquaintances
I can already tell we'll be close soon
Meeting new Mental Illnesses
Who encourage me to stay in
Growing my circle of imaginary world
Shrinking the real one
What would occur if I got my hands on a gun?
I'm alone in my head
And outside of it
Was there a time I wasn't this kind of person?

We are All Theatre Kids Underneath Stage Makeup And
Practiced Pleasantries:
What was I thinking?
Stop romanticizing yourself
And everyone else
People are just ugly People
Line them up on shelves
Mark down their differences
Who's skinny, who's fat
Blonde hair, brunette, black
What talents and knacks do they possess?
In which colors do they choose to dress?
I know, I know I'm blessed
That's easy to forget and hard to remember
Is thinness my best or the size I am now?
How do I leave life without leaving?
Yearn for rest
Is this the worst or has that already passed?
Blast music, Teenager
People leave without saying sorry
Most don't come back
Get used to it
Life has no set cast
Drop the curtain
Get off stage
I didn't audition for the character I'm playing
No one gives us lines to our parts
I stutter after hours of mental rehearsal
Behind the scenes or lead role
I want out of this production
Unzip this costume
Give me a makeup wipe

E.G.

I'm not comfortable here
This building isn't mine.

Listen, I Said Let Me Go:
Do you think it hurts to Love me?
Watching People hurt trying to
Hurts me.

Forearms Are Public Museums For Failure:
How many more times will I cut tonight?
Each slice inches further down my arm
Inches closer to ending my life
This one is from...
This was when...
Oh, the series of slashes?
Everyone notices those
Every movement of the blade
Severs a tie
Goodnight or Goodbye?
Who knows?
Not I
Can a blood infection be worse
Than this infection of my brain?
Multiple mistakes made
God, save me by your grace
I Love my best friend
He'll never be mine
I'd like to try drunk
It has to be better than this
Anything is
I can't eat, I can't eat
It won't surprise me to be left behind
I was never taught how to decline invitations
A hospitable chance to die
Dance across the remains of childhood
I'm slipping away unnoticed, almost
My Mother was younger tonight than I've ever seen her
I want to be as strong as she
I lied instead
A burden is all I am

Trust me to know
I should be dead.

Anorexia:
I don't want Ana to go
Without her I'd be lost
My bones would never show
Couldn't care less of the cost
Frustration and desperation have forced me to be careless
No one heeds my warning
I don't eat
She doesn't know
Focused on everyone that's important
While they're not watching
Of this fat one day I'll finally be free
Do I scare you?
I scare me
My hair isn't falling out yet
Locked inside this shell of fatigue and numbers
I don't think it's possible for me to get dumber
So what if I skipped another meal?
No calories today
That's the deal
Is this happening?
Is it real?
I've made my decision and I won't repeal
I'm shriveling inside and out
The call to dinner is a call to hide
Don't you get it?
I'm way too wide
She likes to say it's pride
They'll never understand how bad it is
Until this is the reason I die.

Aftermath Of Attempt:
14 years old
Clinical Depression
Developing eating disorder
Empty therapy sessions
Social Anxiety
Purple gown
On Suicide watch for 2 days and 12 hours
Camera in the corner of an open hospital room
Not allowed to lock a bathroom door
Not allowed to have shoelaces or hoodie strings
(Bed sheets don't work. I tried)
Pull up your sleeve for a blood test
(Are the pills gone?)
Don't meet your Mother's eyes when she sees what's there
Not allowed to touch a phone
Not allowed to see a friend
Not allowed to leave
(Or later, to stay)
Because you tried to Leave
These are the consequences for what you have done
In the wreckage left from irate winds
In the settling dust of deceitful sorrow
In the aftermath of attempt
Every nearby face asks
Why?
I Don't Know
I know I'm young
I know I'm a Sad that's bigger than Sadness
I know I don't want to be here
Why?
How about this

E.G.

I'll tell you why I tested the chance of suicide
When you can tell me
Why it Failed.

Notice:
If you've made it here
Thank you
If that terrified and sickened you
It should
It is terrifying and sickening

Wait

There is light at the end of this tunnel.

Grey = Searching

Greetings From Grey:
We're trying here
Sometimes we're still Sad
Here is the in between
Here is whatever
Lies in the distance separating
Good and Bad
Sad and Happy
Black and White
Shake off your shoes
Step over what has passed

Journey with me.

What Happens Between Clock Ticks:
One minute they care
The next
I am nothing
There
Snap of fingers
Tick of clock
Blink of eye
Gone
Why did you come here
If you didn't plan to stay?
Why did you Love me
If you knew it wouldn't remain?
Depression is scary
It's left my walls weak and sweating
Please teach me how to not be wary
Paranoia is a helicopter parent peering over both stripped
shoulders
Help Me Run Away
I ask often for guidance from above
I'm still afraid
Of what, I don't know
But it's there
Every time I cut it down
It finds ways to regrow.

King, Queen, Life Is A Joke:
Blood has dried
Tears have been cried
Damage from lies
Why did I survive?
They don't hold all the cards
They don't enforce every rule
Step away from falling
Wage battle against murky blue.

Foresight:
I don't understand what you think you saw in me
I wasn't yet who I was going to be.
(I am still not who I could be.)

E.G.

Once:
Someone who held me in the palm of his hand
Whispered around corners
That I was a chipped cup
Overflowing with a scalding sea.

Once:
Someone said that I didn't feel enough
While simultaneously
Shouting in my opposing ear
That I felt too deeply.

Once:
It was carved into my mind's inner workings
That I was too big on one side
Too small on the other.

Once:
I believed everything I heard
As long as it was a negative connotation
About the way I was or my character.

Helium, Not Hot Air Balloon:
My soul aches for lost ones
I'm not large enough to keep them off the ground
How can I be
When I am not big enough to stand up without assistance?
(Will you take a few minutes out of your day to assist me?)
Bubbly buoyancy is only mine at my best
My best has been hidden behind Anorexic ideology
And downward spirals of Destructive tendencies
Since I turned into a Teenager
I'm getting up now
I will stay on the ground no longer.

Take The Hints, They'll Add Up In The End:
Don't follow my footsteps
Deviate from my lead
Sister, Darling
Depression and swirling, Suicidal rituals
Are not what you were born to be
Brother, Love
Turn to your God and pray to be set free
Have faith that your hollow heart
Will be filled with purpose and meaning.

She Wears Short Sleeves For The First Time Since (She
Doesn't Hear The Gasps She Expected):
How could you not have noticed these scars?
Tokens of Demons I've fought
All is not lost
What are kids charged for freedom?
Pay up
Your innocence is forfeit to fulfill this debt
Self-deprecating sense of humor
Your only way to cope
Everything is fine if you call it a joke.

E.G.

On Belay:
I was buried deep inside myself
I am climbing out
Hold me up
Belay on.

Sew Me up, I'm Falling Out Of Myself:
Skin is a patchwork of faded red memories
Hideous map
Tangible taste of his past
Hanging in folds around his head
Draping off shoulders
Love, Love, Love
You've sealed my tongue to the roof
You've struck me stone blind
You're every song I've ever sung.

Soft Girl:
Everything changes me
Yet I remain the same
Flowing in and out of my name
As often and wild as the tide
A smile just as wide
Malleable mood swings
(Would you do me a favor?)
(Care for me as I do for you?)
Infallibly unstable.

Writers Are Beasts Of Burden:
My soul is heavy to hold
Late at night and
Early in the morning
When I am
Full of tears
Empty of feeling
You don't realize the weight of these letters
That's alright
You have your own toils
That's alright
They are not yours to carry.

E.G.

What Will Be Left When They Fade:
I do not wish the scars to disappear
Because if they did
I would disappear with them
You cannot cut a piece of who I am away
And request me to
Remain whole.

Build A Blockade Between My Heart And My Mind:
When I flood with feeling
My hands still search for
Materials to
Dam up my heart
How do I tell them
Not to pick up the ancient knife?
How do I say
It's alright to be washed clean?

Reverse:
One sleeve rolled up
The other pulled down
Tear in his left eye
Other is dry
One bruised fist
One pure white
Knife against wrist
You were not meant for this
Senseless games
Injuring falseness
We can turn this around
If you want to
We can reverse the direction of the day.

I Am An Acquaintance, Not An Obstruction:
I won't ever hurt myself to obstruct your blade
Friendship shouldn't work that way
But I'm here
I can listen
I'm Here

E.G.

You Have Remained On My Mind:
Beautiful things haunt me
Almost more
Than ugly ones do.

Still Sick Pt. I:
The longing to burn
Still smolders
In the exact center of my chest
It sparks at the slightest
Breath of discontent
A gale is brewing on my horizons.

Heart = Trap:
If I hate you
If I Love you
If you mean anything to me at all
You will be distributed throughout my broken words
And tattered pages of a mind
You will be remembered in every drop of blood
Every waterfall of tears
Each dusty reflection
Every struggling scar
Until I have scattered your silhouette
Into the deepest recesses of my cracked
Wandering soul.
(I can't wash your debris away
When there is no outlet to wash them through.)

Recovery, Remembering:
Don't forget what it's like to drown
But don't ever step back into that opaque water.

Deceit:
One I Love most
My head is not your host
I'm inviting you to leave me alone
I don't trust you anymore.

Every Fork Is A Fork In The Road:
Voices said I should hurt
They told me to starve
But it's my choice
I can choose to pardon myself
Push the burden on another
Or with Sadness part.

E.G.

There Is No Knight Tonight:
She writes words for only the stars to see
Their feedback is filled with silence
Still
Their stares are enough
To halfway satisfy
A deeply lonely soul.

Understanding Understanding:
I recognize damaged
The midnight mirror may not gaze back as bleakly as it used
to
I remember when it did
I know what it is to be strangled by bandages
But to know you'll bleed out if they're unwound
I want to scream at them
I understand you
I am you
You shouldn't scream at damaged things
They wilt under one more voice
They run from another fist
Listen, Honey
They don't need to live inside your head
To Love you
They don't need to see where every spider web was woven
To care.

E.G.

Clean Spaces:
Scars used to form the bars of the prison I imagined I was
trapped in
I've come a long way
Knives aren't wrapped around my throat anymore
I can breathe
Clean air is easier to inhale
And exhale
Than I thought it would be.

Realization:
I am already Home
My body is not a tomb
She and I
Will live to fight another day.

Tipping Point:
Words rest with uncertainty
On the fingertips of my brain
Teetering on the edge of something I've forgotten
Interrupt this writing
I beg every passerby
Do Not Let Me Remember This
Nothing has ever grabbed my shadow
And shredded it as deeply
As the destructive addiction we call Self-Harm has
Nothing has ever choked me as far
As my own fingers jabbing the back of this throat
My own hands around my throat
(I'm sorry, Mother, Friend, I never brought myself to speak of
this out loud)
Backpack straps around a wind pipe
Night sky
Dark woods
Suspect: me
Victim: me
Would-be-murderer: Me
It's been two years
Two years isn't enough distance to forget the sting of hand
sanitizer on my useless tongue
Two years hasn't been enough time to reconcile forfeited
friendship
Two years has not been enough salve to heal these white
wounds
After two years
In my Mind's eye
I still fall to my knees on a forest floor
I'm curled on twigs and crying again

(How long did I lay there?)
Stop going back to that place
I'm sorry
My hands are empty
I don't even have a razor blade for company
Because I swore it off for a best friend who didn't believe I
could
After so many months not trying to
Was this page the one
That is finally too much?
I know what some of you will say
I've said it to myself
You did not live through nights like that
To write pieces like this.

(I'm Sorry, I'm Sorry, I'm Sorry.)
(I'm Sorry, I'm Sorry, I'm Sorry.)
(I'm Sorry, I'm Sorry, I'm Sorry.)

E.G.

Wanderer:
I don't have long sleeves
Or fake smiles to hide in now
I don't know where to go.

Wonderer:
Do I blend into a crowd?
Do these sentences that fall from my mouth mean anything?
Jumping from treetops
Spreading sparsely feathered wings
Show me how to make my Mother proud
The waves Sister made
Still lapping at the shore
In the wake of her beauty
It's hard to see what's in store
Will they laugh because I crave more than ordinary?
Soaring, an open sky
Inhaling clouds and blue
I was nearly gone
Yet here I am
Always yearning to move
One day, someone will not walk away
Remain by my side
Until that comes
I wish you knew
How much I Love you.

E.G.

Still Sick Pt. II:
These things I've forgotten how to feel
Are begging to be remembered
Am I strong enough to keep them out?

Grey:
I am nowhere
I am everywhere
I am trapped in between.

Mood Swings:
People who resemble other People
I don't know where to begin
Girls and Boys who Love each other
In that picture I don't fit in
My emotions change quickly
From fat to thin then back again
When is it my turn to stay happy?
I'm told no one consistently is
But from my Self-Inflicted outsider's post
I see through a different lens.

Misguided:
Here come the lies again
Washing me away
Changing this Girl into a skeleton day by day
Teaching her
Each time you smell food
Run the other way
Thought I was stupid
Wanted to be dead
If I'd known where that path led
I wouldn't have followed it's winding course
Swallowed up in red
Still they wanted more
Couldn't find a door
How to navigate Home?
Starving to bones
It was only God who saved me from the lies that were
wringing me dry
In dingy darkness I no longer roam.

E.G.

Rerouting:
My brain was just beginning
To see in letters and colors
Instead of endless numbers
Why would I ruin everything?
Neither of us have a clue
Where on the map have I walked to?
The key says X marks Recovery
In every direction
The only X's I see
Are the ones criss crossing my arms again and again
Tell me the lane ends with the next red bridge
The rivers are nightmares swimming in irreversible mistakes
The liquid running underneath and over my skin
Terrorizes my legs into weakness
When crimson messes drip from my hips to my knees
I can't run
I can't run
I can't run from Darkness
When it has robbed the blood from my veins
And taken its place.

Ignorance:
We walk through a quaking city
Oblivious to the breaking
Until it becomes our turn to be hurt
Why is it
Kids notice cracks in the sidewalk
And stop to leap over or look
When once they're grown
They forget to remember them
Until it's too late
They trip
Heels are scuffed
Kneecaps scratched
And there's no one to pick them up.

E.G.

Mute Mind:
I haven't learned to speak my thoughts out loud
They find form somewhere between the pencil
And the paper.

Scrapbook:
Surviving on memories
Past in the eyes
Forgotten oaths crunching underfoot
Scotch taped secrets
Middle child
Smallest child
Trouble child
Incomplete.

Come Back:
To see her smile
A miracle
And pitiful that it has come to that
Her Sadness has grown
While I have watched
Held back by
An identical struggle
Isn't it time for her to find her fire again?
Person
Or
Carcass
Once rot sets in
Inside or out
There isn't much to differentiate
Between living
And seeing how long she can last.
(At least as long as I do)
(Please last.)

I Am Not A Relapse:
I am again finding myself
Itching to hold a razor blade or knife
It takes effort and faith
To pick up a bow or pencil
And play or write instead of slice
This is a battle I may fight
The rest of my life
By God's grace
I'll have the strength to put on His armor
To face every dark day and night.

E.G.

Opposable Ideas :

When
Music starts
Do you listen to
The notes
Or
To the silence between the notes ?

His
Eyes spoke loudly
Mine
Were the only pair to shout a reply .

Our Mothers teach us to say goodbye
But who
Shows us how to let go when it's time ?

Light fires around your reflection
It tires me to refrain from Loving .

Always
Turing my gaze above
Pink, gold, blue
Skies are the same color as my mind .

Paths wind through clouds and gusty mountain wind
Lost
Unforgettable, far away
With trees, sun, and stars
I bend and break .

New Day (Dream):
I used to watch blood drip
Subconsciously and consciously searched for a gun
My past self was reckless
(Anything to be numb)
Desperate to be gone before the morning sun
Many days were wasted
Vacant of hope
Nowhere to run
Today
Praise God
I am certain better times have arrived
And there are more to come.

Glass Boxes:
A glass box
No one could hear me talk
Rivulets of tears
Drawing in blood red chalk
Finger gripping soft skin
Twisting
Deceived into thinking there's too much bulk
Mirrors lying
Spark dying
Surrounded by others thriving
There was no way out
Into that mire
You came
Calling my name
Girl, it's alright
I'm not done with you
Step into the light
Release your grip on spite
Pick up your pen
Write.
Since then
When thrown into a crowd
I tend to look for hints of glass boxes
Everybody has one
The glint of walls
Is more capturing
Than blue eyes and
Perfect smiles
I've preferred jade as a romantic shade of gaze
For as long as I can remember
Show me your false personality front

Reveal the similarities that make you unique
I promise to protect every precious piece you allow me to find
Lasting Peace is possible, Love
(Believe me, I used to think it impossible too)
When you anchor it in the Only God.

The Wrong Questions:
Do I Love them enough to balance
The hate turned inward?
Do they Love me?

Tonight:
I'm divine
The Demons are blind
How could anyone cast a cold stare on star shine?
Never mind
I know the answer
One body's lack of appreciation
Does not steal the beauty of a dancer
My world doesn't have to fade
Because you're numb to color
I'm dumb, clumsy, still Alone
Tonight
I don't care
Darling, I'm waiting up for you
Come Home.

Still Sick Pt. III:
Yesterday
I brushed off the ashes of who I used to be
Why am I pulling to rejoin the flames?

Relapse:
I swore I would never do it again
Pick up a blade
Watch the rend of my skin
But I did
Great.
Welcome back to my twisted head, Self-Hate
I wrote that I would never do it again
Get on my knees in front of a toilet and bend
How long has it been?
Who cares?
My throat is sore
Regurgitate one bite more
Gross?
I'm fully aware
I wanted to blend in
No
Whore
If someone sent help I wouldn't complain
But they would tire of me
It's far too deep of a stain to scrub out
Armed only with pity and nice words
These voices inside are stronger than us
And they want pain
Always more Pain
I'm sorry I broke
Please understand how big the strain is
I realize there is nothing of value to gain in these orchestrated
collapses
But I gave in
The conversations in my head steer me further from happy
They've taken over my brain

E.G.

Don't let them in!
I'm hardly trying
Night after night after day they win
Screaming that I need to be thin for permission to grin
Images and numbers swim
When dizziness isn't in control
I'm sorry I'm not fighting like I know I could
I didn't have to let them spin me off course
There are others who have it much worse
You deserve to be happy
If any of us do
Because I was stolen from
I stole that from you.

Suicide Is On The Schedule:
Pretending to be busy
Finding fresh ways to leave
Struggling to find colorful air
Existing to weave stories of other places
I am perpetually restless
I can't stay here.

E.G.

Robbery Is Worse Than Murder:
Please
Someone
Tell me how to silence the voices in my head
I'm alone every night
Except for them
They steal my will to live
Lying in the middle of the bed
Slipping back into the filthy garb of Self-Hatred
On a plate shaped sled
No one but me is haunted by the red
That leaked from my wrists and hips
Taunting, Tempting
It's never enough
You are never enough
I would rather be dead than listen to this torturing racket
another hour
(It isn't true. Don't believe me, I am no longer me)
Monsters see straight through every bluff
(It's no use)
See, they're still vengeful the attempt on my life wasn't their
victory
He disappears every time I turn around
(Who is He?)
Leaving a faint trail of smoke
They never search for me
When I need most to be found
Of course not
You gained another pound
I play a convincing hostess
Opening the door when they knock

Even though I know from last time they tramped inside
without wiping their feet
There's only soiling dark on the other side of the lock
(Don't be angry. My handles are bruised. I am too tired to
hold them off)
Back to the beginning
Now I'll have to start anew
It gets harder to fight each time
Screams say I'm worthless
Only in your dreams would the one you Love look for you
God, tonight the Demons are deafeningly loud.

E.G.

(Please Don't Read This. Please Don't Read This. Please Don't
Read This):
My clean streak is meaningless
In my head
I've slid that knife over my skin so many times
That if these images within were real
I would be ten times dead
I've
Said too much
I'm
Sorry.

Pain Washes In Patterned Waves:
She lay still
Familiar floor
Remembering how it felt
To trip on one's own miserable mistakes
Sinking into revived crimson
Until the sting was all she could call real
Pushing away what could have been salvation
Until she believed she would never be brave again
But she was wrong.
Joy returned on the staff of a song.

Track and Everyone Leaves (Please Don't Take This Title
Seriously):
Waiting for things that will never come
Wasting away
Asking silently
Will you stay?
Or should that be labeled piteous begging?
Since that's what we call a person saying what they really feel
Hating myself
The only action that stirs passion
Yes, Hate is an action
I didn't ask to be this way
I'm not working to not be
If Love is a chase
I am no runner
You crave companionship
But are you brave enough to adore another?
It takes more than being willing
Learn not to expect another to fill your soul
Before you're taught the hard way
Digging holes to hide in with a shovel broken from frequent
use
Stay there
Don't be a bother.

Violinist Falls In Love With Boy:
Feeling artwork
Rain on skin
Wondering if blushing ruby red is a condemnable sin
I haven't bled by my own hand in twelve days
(This doesn't mean I've shelved the urges
Or the pain that causes them)
Murderous toward myself
For my brain can't do everything
And I want it All
Do you think of me as big?
Be honest
The way I was shrinking and now I'm not
I've never stood in the shape of a twig
Swigs from foreign bottles
Blazing toward desensitized numb
Marking yourself for not being flawless
Does that make sense?
Of course not
Knowing doesn't loosen its grip
It doesn't erase scars
Hands stronger than mine-
(What am I saying?)
(Every hand is stronger than mine)
(I would like to hold yours)
Tipsy little girl
Yearning to live lawless
Please, don't whittle away your human realness
Do my pleas hold weight with anything or anyone?
I won't win until they do
Reeling when I stood
This is a vibrato Demonstration on the

E.G.

Fingerboard of a young heart
My sincerest apologies if the pitch is horrendous
I have never had patience to practice
Yet he pulls
I Love you
From me
Again and again.

Glimpse Into Internal Dialogue:

Disappointment bites hard
Irritation is a shard of glass
In my wound of a heart
Why can't I do anything right?
God can't use a depressed freak like me
Shut up! You know that's not right
Yeah, but I want to cut again
Remember the motion?
Forget the distance
Between my last slice and this next one
Should I tell him that I grow or grew?
What's wrong with me?
Where's my happy?
I'm trying, I'm trying
Not to lie and wish once more to be dying
Dying
I was dying last winter
My heart beat too fast
No food stayed with me for a month
It's the truth
Can you believe it?
I thought it was better this time
It was
Is
But, Lord
I need your help to stay afloat in this mire
Please send help, God
The situation is dire.

Give The Reasons Back:
I've found so many reasons to live
But in the moments
When my head and heart begin to pound in discordance with
each other
They are snatched and torn from my grasp
And I'm left
Lost
Reaching
Searching
When does the Finding happen?

Another Conversation Between Me And Myself:

> *He's not here*
> *Did you hear what I said?*
> *He's nowhere near*
> *You threw him away in a moment of fear*
> *He's gone*
> *Why should he return?*
> *You can't even take care of yourself*
> *You wouldn't be able to care for him.*

Wrong
It's easier to Love someone else
Than it is to Love who I'm supposed to be.

> *What makes you think you're worth something?*

Nothing, now he's gone
And you've returned
How did you get back in?
I thought I locked you out-

> *Your thoughts aren't your own*
> *Stand still, Stupid*
> *You can't keep escaping yourself*
> *Through open cuts*
> *And fingers jamming the back of your throat*
> *You are who you are*
> *You're the only one who can choose to quit or keep*

going.

(Please Keep Going.)

Privacy:
Leave my tattered words alone
They're all I have
Forcing your way into these pages
Is the same as cutting off my sleeves
And pointing out my ribbed skin
Get out
Take my words out of your head
They're mine
You can't have them unless I hand them to you
(This is me handing them to you)
(Freedom is in the Choice)
Saying sorry doesn't pull my sentences out of your eyes
It doesn't give back a secret mind
Get out
You can't have Him
What I feel for Him is mine alone
You can't have Him
You can't
Busting up and breaking down walls
Stop it
Scraping my emotions into notebooks
Instead of into my forearms
Does not make them anymore public or ready to be shared
(If you're reading this, they must be ready to share)
Get out.

Round & Round & Round (& Round & Round & Round):
Cut
Bandage
Clean
Repeat
Starve
Eat
Purge
Repeat
Hold it in
Let it out
Cover it up
Repeat
When does this
Violent cycle
Of battering Sadness
End?

Get Through It:
Leaving ink on paper
The same way I left slits on my skin
For many different reasons
It's difficult to stop once I begin
Pencil to paper
Razor blade to wrist
I twist and untwist
I didn't find solace there
I do in this
Am I too young?
I haven't had my first kiss
Whether I run or hide
There are still many sunsets to see
Leftover time to bide
Are you along for Life's ride?
Live and die with the push and pull, pull, pull of tide
Not enough days here to waste more on despising yourself
I think I might
Get through another night.

Tug Of War Mentality:
Too much pressure to be soft and rough
Reassure me I am good enough to be here
I don't think
I'm good enough
For who?
We don't ask that question here.
(We are afraid of the answer.)

E.G.

Don't weigh My Value; I'm Still Scared Of Scales:
Don't lie to me about what you see
I know I don't know my worth
Recovery takes longer than a four syllable word
Healing is a hollow
When you can't find the actions to pair it with
I Love you, Edes
From a little brother is magic
He doesn't know his power
But with one fragmented sentence
Loneliness loses its hold.

Nothing Sounds Right:
What do you see when you look at me?
What do you think when I smile?
I can't find who I am
Haven't seen myself in a very long while
Slowly, slowly, slowly
Moving past nights of knives and cold bathroom tile
I need to lock it all up
Light a match and burn the file
I have your number
Though you told me to lose it
Don't worry
You know me
Too afraid to dial
We'll make it
It'll be alright
I've known for years
That I cannot be the type of person
Who says things they never plan to do
Whatever I'm let loose at
I have to memorize it
I have to make it mine.

Hospital Boy:
Please try to eat
Was the last thing he said
Walked out with his Mother
I haven't seen him since
Did he really believe I could beat the beasts warring in my
head?
I miss him
I do
He'd be disappointed in the lines I drew
Before and after we last talked
He knew I wasn't okay
I knew too
Not everything we said was true
He smiled despite, in spite of surrounding Sad
He cared, and cared, and–
There's no metaphor for this
He cared about People
I would like to be like him
If he's reading this
I hope we meet again
Older
When Suicide has stopped watching us
When we are no longer scar-clad.

Remember :
Panic , frantic
Forcing food the wrong way through your throat
Stop !
It ' s supposed to be one way !

Remember :
Racing , pacing
Breath
Spinning , losing
Vision
Burning , churning .

Remember :
Sadness
Scratched my inside to exterior pink and swollen
I am pleading
Begging
Stay on this side of insanity
Stay beside me .

Midwest Miracle:

Storm like thunder
Cry like rain
Going insane
Inside this hurricane
In which I am
Wind
Water
And Aftermath.

Sprained cyclone
Injured air
Flattened crops of
Who I might have been
Strewn everywhere no one else can see.

Corn field cure
Nature is God's living gift
Where I hide
To hide from discontent.

What I Wanted; What I got:
All we've said and written
Almost didn't happen
Because of the sickness in my head
If when I'd swallowed those pills
I had wound up dead
As I intended to
You wouldn't know me like you do today
Nor would I, you
There would be no sense of dread
Or feelings and complication
It's too late.

Meaning: I'm Still Here

Meaning: It's Not Too Late.

Relapse (Reprise):
No, he's right.
I'm an attention whore.
*Of course he doesn't care that your throat is repeatedly
stripped and sore*
Or that you've relapsed and cut more
Quit using the same rhymes
Don't you have anything new to say this time?
*They'll look at you like you've committed a third degree
crime*
Stop it.
You know they won't
Will they ever?
Shadows have grown tall again
Don't you feel small?
We'll never let you get better
Your cries for help are of no avail
They can't hear you in your head
When you crawl into bed and cry yourself to sleep
We'll be the only company you keep
It only took a few seconds to grab a blade
To break skin and promises together
Bursting a vein fells a bridge connecting me to the will to stay
They made you, didn't they?
No, and that's the worst part
I make my own bad decisions
When you don't use strength you lose it
I am barely crawling from the mess inside
Foresight is useless when all you see is lies
My Demons wield blinders and sledgehammers
I carry a cracked heart.

An Example of Resisting Their Return:
Why am I back to this?
Tell them I don't want to die
Tell them they aren't allowed to have me or haunt me again
Throat too sore
Eyes too wet to dry
Let me be!
I'm better now
I want to cleanse Depression from my pores
Scrub for as long as it takes
To wash away nearly deadly mistakes.

E.G.

Escape Plan:
Get out of my head
You're not permitted under my bed
Do you hear me?
Do you see my mouth move?
Your ways are known here
I choose happiness instead
You will not resurrect my dead
Preserve my graveyard, Please
The ones buried there are buried for a reason
Stop tugging my threads
You can't Unravel me anymore
I've cut out my loose patches
(No More Cutting)
I am a tight knit pattern with no room for interruptions
I'll travel my path
Building it of passions and People I Love
Don't ask how
We're not there yet
This path will lead me Home
Unlike yours
Which is solely interested in misery and showing off sickly
revealed bones
I'm going to see Rome one day
I'll never make it to eighteen if I do what you say
It's too costly a price
I am not in your debt
You haven't caught me
Not again.
(Not Yet.)

Lasting Repercussions:

They still touch me,

> (When they touch me,)

Afraid that I'll break.

> (I am not a glass spider web now.)

I won't let myself be blown away.

> (As if I have control over wind.)

(As if I'm not still fragile.)

> (As if I won't be a writer the rest of my life.)

E.G.

Requiem Or Request:
Wrap your arms
Around my shoulders
Remind me how small and strong I am
I want to leave these wrongs behind
Will you be
A way out
Or is that
Too much to ask ?

A Plea:
Semicolon
Youth stolen
Put down that knife
Now
It's not your friend
I'm telling you
Stop before it starts
Don't
Cut.

E.G.

Pickup Truck With A Purpose (Pick Me Up Soon, I'm Ready
To Leave):
We're almost to the end
Can you see around the bend in the road?
It's time to restart
Key in the ignition
Will you be my ride?
Peace of mind
At Last
The sun has set and faded
We made it through the lonely hours
Sunrise is waving to us
Take heart with me.

White = Finding

A New Chapter:
What is White?
I will tell you
When I find out.

Discover with me.

Choices:
To write about how hard it is to put the knife down
You have to put the knife down.

To Who I Was, To Who I Am:
For a long time
I have made believe to be stitched of scars
Skipped meals
And inky midnight thoughts
That is not what I am made of
I am sewn with a thread of words
Stamped with Jesus Christ's precious Love
Woven of obscure seconds
The poetry found in waves
Resonates with my heartbeat
Broken music
Through God
I am beautiful
I am taking hold of it
I am His and mine
This is what I am made of.

Growth:
Time has passed
The slopes of your skin may never be clear
Of your past and present fear
But they were right, weren't they?
Don't fight the fact that it's gotten better
Are we still stepping blindly?
Voices don't hold your mind quite as tightly
A few pounds heavier or not
Someone Loves you, Darling
Darling, even if you can't make yourself chew today
Or change your color from red to blue
Even if you don't smile as brightly as she does
Even if it's been awhile since you were able to look at your
reflection
With anything other than criticism
Someone Loves you
And there are more someones to come
A clean streak or lack of one
Is not who you can become
Learn to let go of the cage
It takes courage to turn the page and face Demon's rage
The amount of calories you've swallowed or purged
Doesn't solve anything
You'll only grow the urge to damage yourself
Honey, Sweet
Someone Loves you
His name is God.

E.G.

Look Closely, Watch Out:
Poetry is not for the faint of heart
Take your weak searches for belonging elsewhere
I left behind tact when I learned to write
Words have grown from part of me
Into the heart of me
Look out or watch closely
My poorly pent passions
Have grasped the channel they fit through
We're stepping out
Walking on water, on airy light.

What Happens Next:
We are breathed back to life.

E.G.

Touch Tells More Than A Wagging Tongue:
You don't need this book
To hear about
My self-centered younger years
Just read the Braille letters of hopelessness
Etched on my skin
To learn the story
It is not unique
There are many Sad People who have acted on their Sadness
It is not lovely
Even healed
But it's all there
All mine
All His.

A Thought Steals Her Breath:
We won't have scars in heaven
Staring down
At skin marred by wrong choices
(She knows they were the wrong choice now)
Unable to remember what she looked like
Before the world introduced Sad
She smiles.

Saved:
A storm of disguises
Was masking my sight
I couldn't break out
No matter how hard I tried
God reached through
With Him came revealing light
After such time in dim grey
It was a surprise to find something fresh and bright
Faith in Jesus Christ
Makes me brave
I'll never be lost again
Remaining His.

The Beginning Of Change:
We write
Running our experiences through a filter
To find the good
Transforming
We can look at it now
Still sore, still hurting
But healing
We are New.

E.G.

Sun Over Your Shoulder:
It's okay
To trip over stumbling blocks of Sadness
But remember, Dear
There are far better things ahead
Than any you've already had.

Buttercup, It's Time To Move On:
Wading in and out of the deep end
Dreaming of being weightless, blind
Waking up to opportunity
Then I see
Fading sunset
Roaring sea
Break apart ice across eyes
More should come from the air in our lungs
Than sighs of who we wish we would be
There is no magic potion
To fill gaping holes
Tragic childhoods can only be to blame for about three-
fourths
Or half
Of your echoing, empty cup
Fear allows a brush against the brink of life
Holding back
How long will you shrink from the caress of a promise?

E.G.

White Lines:
Watch closely
They spell a story
Of the times I mistook
Being Depressed
For being alone
Step into a churning sea of freezing fear
This culminates when I rediscover Him
Or rather, when I realize He was reaching to me
This is what Love looks like
Anything, everything else pales in comparison
This is a Savior worth serving.

Impressionable:
I ache for People so easily
Is it wrong to be as soft as I am?
We are told not to take People at first glance
But that first glance
Is where stories start
Impressions leave me curious & eager to see more
Dreadlocks, expressive eyes, tattoos, personal touches,
hairdos
Vibrancy, coffee cup in hand, a vacant expression, a visibly
good day
People & People & People
Watching or part of the crowd
I am in Love
With this global community
I am not here for everyone
Everyone is here for me
I have asked my perspective
To ask them to be.

Inspirational Quotes In Marker On My Arm (No More Cuts):
You're right
Life is pointless without purpose
This how I find purpose
This is how I search
How do you?
I have to live like I'm Loved and believe it
Learn to let go when I'm not
Take a night to count stars
Start again when necessary
Make space for a breath
Clear my head of clutter
Never throw away a chance to Love
Solidify the lines that smudged
Mark distinction between
Past, future, present
I'm not spread across them anymore
I am sixteen
I'm here
I am happy to be
Satisfied with learning
Wait and See
Is my anthem
Sadness isn't splitting me apart
Living with energy and substance is nice
Boy, you're not allowed to come back unless it's to stay
You won't steal this next year
Like you've stolen the past two or three
I am becoming
I am a current of growth
I am turning into
The Girl

God has kept waiting
For me to be.

E.G.

Ambition:
Any one of us could be carrying the dormant spark
Of the next revolution
Can you feel the warmth working underneath?
Think about the fires we could start
Imagine the avid arsonists we could be
For our faiths.

True Love:
Your soul is right
When it tells you
There has to be more to life
Than not hating yourself
There has to be a greater reason for existence
Than existing
Honey, there is.
There is more
There is so much more
There is One who planted the first trees
And poured the oceans
There is One who spoke the sun into the sky
One who hears your silent whispers
A creature as beautiful as you
Must have a Creator
The universe on its own
Does not have the power to spin lovely things into orbit
The One's name is God
Darling, He Loves you.

E.G.

Reminder:
People are not made of magic and stardust
People are just People
A few are ugly
Most aren't
Oil paint and flower petals may run strongly in our veins
They cannot be a firm foundation
Symphonies, black and white photography
Gorgeous, so gorgeous
Breathtaking on occasion
They cannot protect from the tides that ebb and flow with
existence
Giving Love means more than giving gifts
(I would rather spend time with you than ask you to spend
money on me)
Rifts are not mended by a simple sorry
Halt your senseless words
Show your feelings with action
Shower them with sunshine
Be impossible to forget in every good way
Smile, Honey
It might brighten someone's day
Wield pencils and spears easily in turn
Or forego both to hold a friend's hand
What is going to last in the end?
Not those calories
Not that wrong note
Who will stay?
The ones who are meant to
Be bold
Honey, use your fire to warm the cold.

Friendship (Revised):
You are wrong
I did not lose my grip
I did not slip off an edge
You
Let go.

E.G.

Heal With Me:
You are brave and beautiful, my Darling
The bones under your skin don't need to show
If they steal your naturally given lovely
Rewire yourself away from the idea that skinny is all that
means anything
Cleanse your veins of poison
Rinse it from your hair
Bid goodbye to burning scratches
Raw throats from unheard cries
You've come far
I know it's hard, Dear
I saw you
When your smile split air
Your filled spaces between
Forgot to fasten your coat
Something sparkled that night
Was it you?
I've seen it again and again
When you don't know how bright you are
And I know what it means when you whisper
I'm fine
What's on your wrist doesn't have to be your future
I Love you, Darling
I hear the cries for help
I'm doing everything I can
Please Don't Jump
The genesis of change is reversing the will to die
Bumps in the road do smooth out eventually
Catch me when I fall
Is all I allow myself to ask
Is it too taxing of a task?

Resurrection Is A Miracle:
My smiles are ghosts of lies
No longer
I Am Alive
& Glad Of It.

E.G.

To Still Sad Ones:
It matters that you're starving yourself
The number on the scale does not
It matters that there are scars lying like potholes and cracks
on a country road
In your skin
Being thin, or anything other than what you were designed to
be
Does Not
It matters that you're Sad
Dearest, I've been where you are
Trapped inside yourself
It's not safe behind those bars
Carving your thighs and wrists to ribbons
Fitting into those clothes is not worth it
Not if it takes your life
Grief clings like a cobweb
You can't shake it off
I know
Following the voice's orders encourages more hurt
Hollowing spaces between your collarbones and sanity
Stop it.
They need you here
I need you here-
Maybe, I'm wrong
I've stayed up too long writing one poem out of millions
Tell me, if your ears refuse every other word
Unstop them this once
I want to hear your real laughter again, Friend
If anything I create matters
It has to be this.

(I Am A) Scattered Artist:
I don't fit neatly into boxes
I have yet to find a container in my shape
Slim down
Trim dead ends and excess sides
No.
Let me be messily me
Toss lock and keys
Colors drip freely
Paint with brush strokes big and small
Love how you're made whether it's short or tall
Enthrall kingdoms, crowds, or just one
Work hard until a task is done
Many have come and gone
If you miss someone, call
(I can tell that to anyone but myself
Perhaps it's best that way
Calling wouldn't make me older
Or him more emotionally mature
Still, maybe someday-
I've diverted from the main theme again
I apologize
Everything reminds me of him)
To return to the former strain
Applause or none doesn't change your worth
Always, Always, Always
Remember
The only thing I can remember
God Loves you
He gave His Son to set you Free.

E.G.

Death Is Too High A Price To Pay For Numbers On A Scale:

Scars tracing the curves of my hips
Venomous lies sticking like sugar to soft lips
Time and tissues wasted on a Boy
Who made too many promises to keep
He let them slip.
(He made her Love Him)
(He forgot about her after.)

Worry spent
On a Girl
Who wrote songs about smoking and loss
Eyes gloss over
Words crack skin like a whip
Hope fades with sunset
Noose swings from rafters.

Don't mention oil spills
They shimmer from the right angle
But they stain,   stain,   stain
End the games Starvation is playing with you
She'll catch up if you aren't careful
Your life is not something to bet.

Abandon stale, tangled headspaces
Air was not breathed into your lungs to be rationed
Be fair to yourself
Please, Boy, Girl
There is no reason to skip dinner again
It is not an accomplishment to hear static.

When Love Begins

As visible ribs are not a brand of Anorexic
Hidden ones do not jump to the conclusion that you have
failed
No matter what the caves in your mind whisper
Death is too high a price to pay for numbers on a scale.

I know what you're thinking
I've been there
But it could it possibly be
That Love is sincere this time?
Could you allow the chance of it being real?

Listen when your ears give a pause and let you
Or tell them to Shut Up
You are not owned by the crooked lock on your heart
Break it, Honey
Allow yourself to taste Freedom
Found in The Redeemer
Who died that you may Live.

God > Therapy:
It's a hard fight to stay above Depression
Raise your chin, Love
God is infinitely more powerful than a therapy session
Heart open
Eyes taking in the beat
Stay in the world without falling in stride
With Society's twisted lies
What you wear doesn't make what you are unless you let it
Find where you belong and anchor yourself there
Razor blades and empty stomachs
Are not weapons
Only with God in my heart
Can I fight this
Swallow my pride instead of pills
Let down my walls, not my standards
Whisper
The right ones will hear me
I am tired of living
But my race isn't done
Sixteen can be called a joke or a haze
After the past four years
I can outlast the remaining time
You'll find it hard to faze me.

Emanate:
There's a blaze in my heart
For the Lord who saved me from myself
Can you feel it?
Hear me out
I am in a state of thankful adoration
I will not be silent.

Fourth Floor (World):
I knew in flashes between Suicidal sessions
And diagrams of Depressed brains
I would not stay where I was
I knew I could not stay
A person of regret
Sessions with a shrink
Twice a day
Shoelaces weren't allowed
Can a mentally stable person
Guess why ?
I wonder
Psychiatric hospital ward
For a week and a half
Changes one's view of the world
When all you see of it
Is all you can see from a fourth floor window
Returning
That evening was hard
Back among friends
Away from acquaintances
Without the understanding
That I didn't eat
Returning
Was more difficult than going
The unknown
From the dreaded known
Which do you prefer ?

Asleep Is Too Quiet A Place For This Restless Mind To Rest:
I'm too tired to be here.
Here:
Alive. Awake. Asleep. A-
I can't think of another A word
The titles of my poems sound like punk rock songs and
I don't care
I'm running out of teenage years to fight with
Lord, help me use every day for you
I have so much
I'm done pretending I don't
Childish uncertainty was necessary last week
Now it exhausts me
Being raised on a verbal rollercoaster
Leaves no time to experience vertigo
I will not continue the cycle of this abusive ride
I know who I am
Shuffling feet and blushing giggles
Aren't cute anymore
I'm tired of looking for myself
I'm right here
Prepared my pencils for battle
They're louder than my vocal chords
This is a Girl in Love with her Savior
Ready to serve Him
I leave the restless leaves of youth tonight
Goodbye.

Two Years Ago:
Was Suicidal
Denying the necessity of reliance on God
The Boy's color
Was not the heaviest one in my head
(That came later)
I do not miss Depression's obsession with Death
There were many kind, loyal People
(They outweigh the ones who were not)
Because I willfully forgot how to speak then
I say this now:
I am sorry I don't show more gratitude to you for Staying
When you did
(If you did)
Thank you for waiting for me
To realize
These pages
Not those late Friday night notes
Are what I was saved to share
You are part of the reason
You are reading these words and not those
Thank you.

Today:
To burn or not to burn
Make a choice and choose your life
I have decided to burn
Let passions catch afire
To match the brightest blaze nearby
This glow doesn't emanate from my patchwork heart
I am mirror, pane of glass
Look into me
Find God beating in a once cold chest
Look through me
See Him behind this explosion
Where has the spark of youth gone?
Where does it come from now?
(See it, see it, please see it)
Peer into the window of a healing soul
Trace your finger up this arm
Dodge the ditches and hillocks of last year's deceit
Find me Now
It is not my history
That struggles to remain on my wrists and hips
It is the museum of every
Lost, stained
Ruined, molested
Unchangeable, damaged
Bruised silhouette
(Know this for what it is)
Underneath labels
Over the diagnosis
Past the rubble and wreckage of sore throats
Diets, failed relationships, and lies
See the Devil where he is

Fight him with everything the Lord gave you
Wage war against awful
Know that
With Christ
There is no way we cannot win
The spark of youth is buried
Dust them off
And give them a weapon
This is mine
What is yours?

Foundation:
Watch it, Honey
Don't slip now
You're on solid ground
With your Savior and friends
Once food enters your mouth
It must remain
You're here for a reason
Forget regret
Live without looking back.

Ruination Is Much Easier Than Healing:
I thought I needed to expand White
There should be more happy, right ?
Wrong
This is my life
Past to present
I won't fake or force what hasn't happened
Future songs are on their way
Faint strains approaching
Measures will write themselves when they're ready
They aren't ready today
Suicidal or musical
Where did I put those notes ?
Struggle
Starved
Sworn
I'm pretty sure
(Not entirely sure. He doesn't like when I assume. I don't
blame him. No one likes assumption)
He's moved on
I haven't
(Yet)
Patches of used and reused skin
Call an exterminator to flush these infested thoughts
Crowding pages flutter in swarms
It's not nice
It's not neat
It's me
Flipping through these pages does not deliver a pretty image
so
God, bless whoever reads this with a beautiful week.

Confession; Question:
I admit
I am hesitant to reveal
The depths of hopelessness I landed in
Will it be too much?
Must I show it
Because it is honest
And real?
Godlessness survival
Is the worst I have ever been
Surely
Sharing that must mean
Something
Writing for myself
Or for someone I hope will return
Why was I given this task?
We will have to
Wait & See
What tomorrow brings.

Gratitude:
These poems have never been on purpose
I didn't look at my stuck, withering self and tell me to write
A taste for paper with a dash of pen
Was born on a younger night
It wasn't until nearby in time
My words discovered a seriousness that weighed enough to
notice
These words have matured since the first time they
experienced rain
Sunshine has grown them tall
There's height left to reach
This crop sometimes feels too abundant to have come
From a girl so small
But they did
Here Am I
Ready to be sent
I planted this
The seed came from God
It's of His Glory and Grace
I'm able to
Spell, see, and walk.

Friend:
I'm sorry I don't have more to say
When I know before asking
It was another bad day
I Love you
I hate seeing you Sad
You have more than this
Get Out Of Your Head
You're where the Lies want you
Miserable, alone
The only answer I know is
Learn how to tell your Demons
No
Friend, you aren't hopeless
I know you're not okay, but remember
There are a million People out there
None Of Them Are You
I can't tell you too many times
Friend, better things are coming your way
If you can make it through this wait
To see what's ahead
I promise, I swear
There Is More To Life
Than making jokes about how you wish you were dead
You half mean them, as most teens do
It scares me that our generation is already on one knee in
defeat
Stand Up
We have what it takes to thrive
We have ideals, dreams of greatness
Seize them, Friend
You can get through this

E.G.

I didn't plan to write tonight, but
When my world is in His hands
This is what happens
I know this isn't an answer to all your questions
And I won't say
Whatever works for you
Because there is such a thing
As universal truth
Wrong cannot be right
God is God
An Absolute Absolute
There is no other true, constant, Loving light.

Garden:
An Iris, Lavender, Violet, and Mother
Are lovely
Every time of day, almost every angle
A purple petal for each corner of this backyard garden
But a Dandelion Girl
Does not belong near Home
She was grown to leave
Her childhood blew out of reach before it had time to root
Where could she stand in this graveyard of a square foot plot?
Remembering from 7 to 12 is a lost cause
(Please let me call it that. I must have lost the key to those
years for a reason)
I am not Staying here
I'd choose plane tickets over paying rent
Wanderlust is not a broad enough word to scan the horizons I
want to live
But my future's view changes nearly as often as my moods
Puffed out cheeks and blew Sadness away.
(I would wish for you, if I could.)

Christian:
God Is More Than A Name On A Page
There is more to this writing
Than my own selfish story
I am a teenager
Saved by God's Amazing Grace
Because of Jesus Christ's salvation
I don't have to turn to
Starving or harming myself
Anymore or ever again
If you're going to read this
Wait for the end
More resides in me
Than my insignificant self
I won't say I'm not beautiful another day
Because I am
But only when washed clean
In His gift of perfect Love
Mine is a small story
Compared to the millions around
But I'm thankful for every
Sunrise and sunset that pass
Grateful God has granted me
A second chance
To appreciate being who He made me to be.

Parallel:
Red
Pink
White
Black
Grey
White
Scars and words are the same in my tongue
Instruments and language sound identical in my eager ears
Love like this
Is not Love like that
This Man
Is not him.

E.G.

Honesty:
It takes a deep breath and a patch of sunshine
To face what is left of childhood without a sob
The empty spaces remaining on these forearms
(They will remain empty)
Align with the ones in my head's photo album
(I hope they remain empty)
Gaping holes where memories should be
There's a lot I can't write about
Because there's a lot I can't remember

Here is what I do:

Evenings fade into nights. He is still shouting.
Little sleepy heads.
Shh, don't say anything to make him mad.

Older sister is in charge. Hours later, older Sister is still in
charge.
Why is Dad angry this time?
Three months.
Where is Dad?

Unfinished trailer room. Toolbox instead of hope chest.
Older Sister says
Stay in here with me.

Cracked cement driveways. A summer day chasing ants.
Undercooked green beans.
If you put too much salt on them you won't have to eat it.

A 6-year-old does not understand what family is when she does not see one.

Best friend's house.
She likes her daddy? She respects her daddy? Her daddy came Home and didn't yell?

At the beginning of this piece I was thinking only of the bad, but if the good doesn't belong next to these salvaged pictures, then where does it go?

There was swimming.
I'm proud of you. You don't panic in water.
There was throwing my little brother in the deep end.
My brother was not as calm as I.
What can we say? He will be angry if we try to stop it.

Planting annual gardens. We weighed as much as the dirt bags. We were the ones who carried them.

There were pretentious mealtime prayers when guests were over. I have always hated his company voice.

There were long, long days. He has always worked hard to support us.

The first time he saw my youngest brother was when I took him a photo on his weekend. My youngest brother doesn't know this.

When the weekend cycles ended, things were better. For a month or two.

E.G.

Watching my Mother talk to her Mother in hushed tones with teary eyes. I have wondered many times if things would have been different were my Grandfather still alive.

There was shouting. Shouting and shouting and shouting and shouting and shouting.

There was too much to keep contained in a little Girl's head. There was too much to want it contained.

I look at him now, though sometimes I don't want to. My father has been an angry man longer than I have been alive.

He is still my father.

I refuse to carry a bouquet of regret to his future funeral.

There is too much anger to forget.
There is not too much to forgive.

The Colors Of Now Are Prettier To Dress In:
If she's left Depression behind
If she's abandoned Self-Harm
If Anorexia sits underfed and alone
In the middle of the road
She is finished traveling
If she's stepped out of and shed those costumes
Who is she now?
Musician
Writer
Christian
Sometimes she leaves things unsaid until they're the last left
When they should be first
(She's promising herself not to do that this time)
She thinks
If they hear my hints maybe I won't have to say it
(Lord, give her the bravery to say it)
She knows
If one word is all she's left
It must be
Lord
If a single sentence is allowed
It must be
Jesus Christ is King
If she says one more thing about herself
(As if she hasn't said enough about herself yet)
It must be
She is a Christian
Then
She is a musician because she is a Christian
Then

E.G.

She is a writer because she is a Christian.
(I am She.)

Destination:
Where am I now?
I am on my way to growing up
What have I found?
White trumps grey trumps black
Mostly
Most importantly
God is Everything
And Everything
I need
Is in Him
This wasn't my story
This was
Is
His.

E.G.

Him:
My best friend is so much
I'm doing my best
With every
Goodnight
And
Don't stay up too late
To show him what he means
He's doesn't hear me
Drowned out
His thoughts sound like mine did
When I was endlessly, seemingly endlessly, searching
I want to tell everyone trapped in their head
This is not how you have to be
But This Is
As Loud
As My Voice
Gets
(So far)
He's not happy
He knows I can tell
I don't know
His reply when asked
Why?
He's been snared in lies
Vision clouded
Doesn't that sound familiar
Insecurity is the lifestyle of too many
God, what do I have that can be used?
How do I help?
What do I do?

A Reassurance Paired With A Few Unanswered Queries:
I never once blamed you, Friend
Or thought of you ill
For walking away that night
Summer dusk stars
Late evening trees
To be honest
(I have not always been)
I didn't realize I wasn't alone
Too busy realizing I was alone
A visit to gravel parking lots
(I miss you lots. I say it whenever, as much as I can)
A letting loose of my torn, tired soul
To be honest
(Remember, a mentally ill mind likes it when you lie, even if
you're no good at it)
I have been told I'm Sad for show
Don't you think
If that were the case
My Depression would be conscientious enough
To leave
Or let me know ?
If it's here for looks
Shouldn't it
Pick up the pace
Perform a few magic tricks
Make me a beautiful, Sad girl
Instead of a pathetic one ?
Scatter me in snowfall
Collapse me on stage
Instead of
Attacking me with stealth

In isolated back halls ?
You're not at fault for thinking I was insane
I was, in a way, insane
What else can the possession of a person's personality be
called ?
It's madness
A ramble
Deeper than a run out of luck
Getting better is a gamble
Hard to know what will work
(Sorry, Love, the answer wasn't in your Love)
(That isn't your fault)
Nothing happens without effort
Turns out
God
And trying
Is what it took.

How I Learned To Write:
Some of the strongest People I know can be torn down with
words
Mother, You are the strongest person I know
Sorry doesn't cover the times and ways I have hurt You
Swords cannot defend against selfish, careless slips of the
tongue
Words, even the ones I learned from You
(Sacrifice, Kindness, Courage)
Do not touch conveying the ways I Love You
You are All I can hope to become
(With, of course, my own twist)
I know You aren't perfect
(In no world is there a Mother or child who is)
You are my Mother
I Love You
(For so, so, so much more than Your cooking)
A page simply could not
Be long enough of a letter
To thank You for my childhood
The prettiest parts of me
Were planted and watered by Your consistent hands
I learned to write
Watching You live.

E.G.

Truthfully:
I will not tell you
You are beautiful
If you are as I have been
And hardly trying to be
If looking for blind reassurance that all you need is yourself
If hoping for peace of mind
In a stagnant place
Is why you read poetry like mine
I'm sorry
(I am not apologizing for not saying what I don't believe)
You will not find it here
I've tried treading that path
It was one of the most uneven I have walked
After believing so many lies
I can't make myself sell you one
After escaping a lost battle barely breathing
I will not point you in the direction of defeat.

Nautical Nuances Of The Pen:

Entry 1:
Climbing rigging to the shelves in my brain
I have been a ship lost on the Sea of Confusion
I have been a sailor tossed overboard
Both call me directionless
Both have been true
Main mast has toppled
This hull was split
The galley was flooded
Cargo afloat
Saltwater drowned my sextant and spare dingy
I have been a sinking boat.

Entry 2:
When Love Begins
Is a logbook of the unnamed islands
The teenage years stranded me on
I am weathered for a Girl of almost seventeen
Leathery hands and bound up calf
Low tide pulled me into the depths of Depression
No almanac could have told my 10-year-old self what to
expect of growing up
High-tide washed me onto a land of unexpected expectations
without fresh water
To choke of thirst next to an ocean
To drown in the basement of a house whose foundation is
built in a desert
Irony is an repetitive guest.

Entry 3:
I am pulled apart
I am mended
Waterlogged and sullen
Or wrung out and healthy
Open sea adventures
Were destined to call me
The Writer of my story dictated sooner rather than later
When will the chance to journey penetrate your daily tasks?

Entry 4:
Having seen how harpoons of worry hit People
I have learned to dodge them
Viewing the world through a telescope of tunnel vision
I have learned to throw out visual assistance
And step into life relying on my own feet.
Tanned shoulders prove to give protection from sorrow and
sunburn
Collected exotic artifacts and previous experiences with
Anxiety
Let me know
I already have the beads and battles under my belt
To move on from this place
Tribal scimitars or a Christmas gift from a naive friend
Neither is allowed to touch me again
No matter how comfortable their handles are to hold
I will not grow old in their draining company.

Entry 5:
These cabins are emptied and refurbished
Lord, we're ready to set sail

Send me where the People need the weapons and words you
have packed my childhood with
Show me the reason
I have already half memorized maps to patience and loss
Lord, You are my anchor and lighthouse
You have protected me from cliff faces and his
Set my course, Jesus Christ
Lead this vessel through the waters You choose to help me
through.

Entry 6:
You are the Only true ballast
I have the tools to bail out unwanted weight
You have pulled me over every crest and thunderclap
Remind me to pick up Your strength and use it
Roll these words into a glass bottle and push them
To the soul who is waiting for them
To the soul searching to be new.

E.G.

Apology Letter; Thank You Note:
Fresh starts
Freedom's blue skies or Depression's grey
I'm relearning
How to be alive and like it
Thank you
Brother, Sister, Mother, Friend
For waiting for me to find the road back to happy
I am sorry
You had to sit at the table while I turned away from meals
with a closed mouth
While I kneeled on bathroom floors, dying to be rid of myself
I thought if I were poured out enough times
If I just stayed empty enough
I would disappear
I did not
Thank you
For seeing me
When all I saw was the futile uselessness
Of forcing my body to fit a mold I was not created for
Thank you
For Loving me, and Loving me, and Loving me
I am sorry
You ruined nice clothes, nice days
Wading after me through rapids of doubt and crippling lies
To make sure I wouldn't drown
(Myself)
Thank you
If you are one who stayed
For Staying with me.

When Love Begins (I End):
When Love begins
When Love ends
Does Love have a beginning
Or an end ?
I am starting to see
Love is a constant
An Always, Always
We have only to open our eyes
And look
In its beautiful face
To know.

Look with me.

-   E.G.